PRETZELS
Cookbook

Printed in the USA by G&R Publishing Co., Waverly, IA

Published and distributed by:

507 Industrial Street
Waverly, IA 50677

ISBN-13: 978-1-56383-159-1
ISBN-10: 1-56383-159-7
Item #3718

Let's Twist

Hot Pretzels the Real Way

1 C. water
2 tsp. butter or margarine
1 tsp. sugar
½ tsp. salt
3 C. all-purpose flour

1½ tsp. yeast
4 C. water
5 tsp. baking soda
Coarse salt (kosher or sea)

Put first six ingredients in bread machine pan and set for dough cycle or mix in a mixer with a dough hook until dough forms. Cut dough into 18 strips and roll into ropes. Shape into pretzels, cover and let rise 45 minutes. Bring 4 cups water and 5 teaspoons baking soda almost to a boil in non-aluminum pan. Gently place pretzels into water for about 1 minute, turning once. Remove pretzels and place on greased baking sheet. Sprinkle with coarse salt and bake at 475° about 12 minutes.

Hot Pretzels Shortcut

1 lb. frozen bread dough, thawed   1 T. water
1 egg white   1 tsp. kosher (coarse) salt

Coat two large rimmed baking sheets with non-stick cooking spray. Cut the dough into four equal pieces. On a lightly floured surface, roll each piece into a 24˝ rope, form into a pretzel shape and place on the baking sheets. In a small bowl, beat together the egg white and water, brush over the top of each pretzel. Sprinkle evenly with salt. Loosely cover with plastic wrap and set aside in a warm place to rise for 15 minutes. Preheat oven to 350°. Remove the plastic wrap and bake for 15 to 17 minutes or until golden. Serve warm.

Note: For a little variety, top these with minced onion or garlic salt instead of coarse salt.

Soft Pretzels

3½ C. all-purpose flour, unsifted
2 T. sugar
1 tsp. salt
1 pkg. active dry yeast
1 C. water

1 T. margarine
1 T. water
1 egg yolk, beaten
Coarse salt

Mix 1 cup flour, sugar, salt and undissolved yeast. Heat 1 cup water and margarine to 120° to 130°. Gradually add to dry ingredients; beat 2 minutes at medium speed of mixer. Add ½ cup flour. Beat at high speed 2 minutes. Stir in enough additional flour to make a soft dough. On floured board, knead 5 minutes. Set in greased bowl; turn to grease top. Cover and let rise in warm, draft-free place 40 minutes. Divide dough into 12 equal pieces. Roll each into a 20″ rope. Shape into pretzels or other shapes. Place on greased baking sheets. Cover and let rest 5 minutes. Mix egg yolk and 1 tablespoon water; brush on pretzels. Sprinkle with coarse salt. Bake at 375° for 15 minutes or until done. Cool on racks.

Olive and Garlic Pretzels

20 kalamata olives (about ¾ C.), pitted
1 anchovy fillet
1 T. chopped garlic
2 T. olive oil
Fresh ground black pepper
1 pkg. active dry yeast
2 T. sugar
2 T. vegetable oil

1½ C. warm milk (110°)
4 to 4½ C. all-purpose flour
1 tsp. salt
1 slightly beaten egg white
1 T. water
1 T. kosher salt
1 C. Creole mustard

Combine the olives, anchovy, garlic, olive oil and black pepper in a food processor and process until the mixture is smooth, about 15 seconds. Set aside. Combine the yeast, sugar and 1 tablespoon of the oil in the bowl of an electric mixer fitted with a dough hook. Add the milk. With the mixer on low speed, beat the mixture for about 4 minutes to dissolve the yeast. If the yeast mixture doesn't begin to foam after a few minutes, it means it's not active and will have to be replaced. Add the flour, salt and olive mixture to the yeast mixture. Mix on low speed until it lightly comes together, then increase the speed to medium and beat until the mixture pulls away from the sides of the bowl,

(continued on next page)

forms a ball and climbs slightly up the dough hook. Remove the dough from the bowl. Coat the dough with the remaining teaspoon vegetable oil. Return the dough to the bowl and turn it to oil all sides. Cover the bowl with plastic wrap, set in a warm draft-free place and let rise until doubled in size, about 2 hours. Remove the dough from the bowl and turn it onto a lightly floured surface. Preheat oven to 350°. Roll the dough into 12 x 10″ rectangle. Cut into 20 strips, 12 x ½″. Gently pull each strip into a rope about 16″ long. To form the pretzels, cross one end over the other to form a circle, overlapping about 4″ from each end. Take one of the ropes in each hand and twist once at the point where the dough overlaps. Carefully lift each end across to the edge of the circle opposite it. Tuck the ends under the edges to form a pretzel shape. Lightly moisten the ends with water to seal completely. Place the pretzels on the prepared baking sheet. Bake for 5 minutes. Remove from the oven. Bring 1 gallon of salted water to a boil. Add several of the pretzels at a time in the boiling water. Cook for 2 minutes on each side. With a slotted spoon remove from the water. Drain on paper towels. Bring the water back to a boil and repeat the cooking process. Regrease the baking sheet. Place the pretzels on the baking sheet. Whisk the egg whites and water together. Using a pastry brush, brush each pretzel with the egg wash. Sprinkle each pretzel with the kosher salt. Bake for 20 to 25 minutes or until golden brown. Remove from the oven and serve warm with Creole Mustard.

Oatmeal Raisin Cookie Pretzels

1 C. (2 sticks) unsalted butter
¾ C. white sugar
¾ C. brown sugar
2 eggs
2 C. all-purpose flour
1 tsp. salt

1 tsp. ground cinnamon
1 tsp. baking soda
2 C. oatmeal
1 tsp. hot water
1 C. raisins
2 tsp. vanilla extract

Preheat oven to 350°. Grease a cookie sheet and set aside. Add butter and sugars into a mixing bowl and cream with mixer. Add the eggs and mix well. With a large spoon, mix in the flour, salt, cinnamon, baking soda and the oatmeal. Mix well. Add the water, raisins and vanilla. Flour a workspace and with a rolling pin or your hands make a "snake" with the dough and cut it into several pieces. Form into a pretzel shape. Place on the prepared cookie sheet. Bake for 10 to 15 minutes (depending on how thick your snakes are). Let them sit and cool on the stove.

Chocolate Pretzels

½ C. butter or margarine
¼ C. sugar
1 large egg, beaten
1 tsp. vanilla extract
¼ C. milk
¼ C. cocoa

2 C. flour, unbleached, unsifted
FROSTING:
2 T. cocoa
1¼ C. confectioners' sugar
2 T. butter or margarine, melted
½ tsp. vanilla extract

Cream ½ cup butter and the sugar until light and fluffy. Beat in the egg, vanilla and milk. Sift cocoa and flour and mix into butter mixture until thoroughly blended. Chill dough until firm enough to handle (about 30 minutes). Using 2 tablespoons dough, roll a rope about 12″ long between your hands. Shape into a pretzel as follows: Make a loop about 1½″ in diameter by crossing the ends, leaving 1″ tails. Flip the loop down over the crossed ends. Press firmly into place. Place pretzels on greased baking sheets. Bake at 350° for about 10 minutes.

FROSTING: In a small bowl, mix cocoa and confectioners' sugar. Gradually stir in butter and vanilla. If frosting is too thick, thin with milk. When pretzels are cool, spread with cocoa frosting.

7

Breakfast Pretzels

¾ C. dried blueberries,
  or other dried fruit
2 T. sugar
4 T. vegetable oil, divided
½ tsp. cinnamon
1 pkg. active dry yeast
2 T. sugar

1½ C. milk
4 to 4½ C. all-purpose flour
½ tsp. salt
1 slightly beaten egg white
2 T. water
1 C. honeyed cream cheese,
  for spreading

Place the blueberries, sugar and 1 tablespoon of vegetable oil in the bowl of a food processor and pulse to make a thick paste. Grease a large baking sheet with 1 tablespoon of oil and set aside. Warm the milk in a small saucepan to 110° and set aside. Combine the yeast, 1 tablespoon of sugar and 1 tablespoon of oil in the bowl of an electric mixer fitted with a dough hook. Add the milk to the bowl and with the mixer on low speed, beat the mixture for 4 minutes to dissolve the yeast. Add the flour, salt and blueberry paste to the bowl, and mix on low speed until it begins to come together.

(continued on next page)

Increase the mixing speed to medium and beat until the dough pulls away from the sides of the bowl and forms a tight ball, about 2 minutes. Oil a large mixing bowl with 1 tablespoon of oil. Remove the dough from the mixer and place it in the oiled mixing bowl, turning to lightly coat with oil. Cover the bowl with plastic wrap or a damp kitchen towel and set in a warm, draft-free place. Let the dough rise until doubled in size, about 2 hours. Remove the dough from the bowl and turn it onto a lightly floured surface. Roll the dough into a 12 x 10″ rectangle. Cut the dough with a sharp knife into 18 pieces (about ¼ cup each). Gently roll and pull each one into a long thin ribbon, about ½″ in diameter and 14″ in length. Bring the ends up to form a U-shape and twist to form a wreath, bringing the ends down and across as though making a bow, pressing down to seal the ends. Preheat oven to 400°. Bring a large pot of water to a boil and add the pretzels in batches of 6. Cook, turning once, about 2 minutes on each side. Remove from the water and drain on paper towels. Combine the beaten egg with 2 tablespoons of water. Brush the pretzels with the mixture and sprinkle with a combination of the remaining sugar and ½ teaspoon cinnamon. Place on the prepared baking pan and bake until golden brown, 20 to 25 minutes. Remove the pretzels from the oven and serve warm with honeyed cream cheese.

Pineapple-Pretzel Salad

2 C. crushed pretzels
⅓ C. sugar
½ C. butter
1-8 oz. pkg. cream cheese

½ C. sugar
1-8 oz. tub whipped topping
1-20 oz. can pineapple tidbits,
    drained

Mix pretzels, ⅓ cup sugar and butter. Put in 9 x 13″ pan and bake at 400° for 7 minutes, stirring occasionally. Cool. Blend together cream cheese and ½ cup sugar. Fold in the whipped topping and pineapple. Chill for 2 to 3 hours. Stir pretzel mixture in just before serving.

Pineapple-Pudding-Pretzel Salad

2 C. crushed pretzels
1 C. butter, melted
1-8 oz. pkg. cream cheese
1 C. white sugar

1-8 oz. container frozen whipped
  topping, thawed
2-20 oz. cans crushed pineapple
½ (3.4 oz.) pkg. instant vanilla
  pudding mix

Preheat oven to 350°. Place crushed pretzels in the bottom of a 9 x 13″ baking dish. Pour melted butter carefully over top. Bake in preheated oven for 10 minutes. Cream together cream cheese and sugar. Fold in whipped topping. Spread over cooled crust. Combine pineapple and pudding mix. Spread over whipped topping layer. Chill until serving.

Snickers Bar Salad

6 Delicious apples
4 Granny Smith apples
6 Snickers bars

16 oz. whipped topping
Pretzels, crushed

Dice apples, leaving peelings on. Cut up Snickers bars. Mix in whipped topping. At serving time, put crushed pretzels on top.

Cream Cheese Fruit Salad

2 pears, chopped
2 apples, cored and chopped
2 ripe bananas, sliced
1 pt. fresh strawberries, sliced
3 C. seedless grapes
½ lemon, juiced

8 oz. fat-free strawberry cream
 cheese
½ C. packed light brown sugar
2 tsp. vanilla extract
½ T. ground cinnamon
1 C. fat-free pretzels, broken

Combine the pears, apples, bananas, strawberries and grapes. Add lemon juice and toss. Blend together the cream cheese, brown sugar, vanilla and cinnamon; add the fruit and pretzels. Fold together. Serve immediately with a dollop of lite whipped topping or refrigerate until chilled.

Crunchy Chicken Salad

2½ C. cooked and diced chicken
1 tsp. salt
1 small can pineapple tidbits, drained
1 C. diced celery

1⅔ C. green grapes, cut in half
⅔ C. salad dressing
⅔ C. whipped topping
1 C. pretzels

Mix all ingredients EXCEPT the pretzels in a serving bowl. Right before serving, stir in the pretzels. This can be made up the night before.

Twists on Main Dishes

Tuna Casserole Crunch

1½ C. uncooked wide egg noodles
1-6 oz. can water packed tuna,
  drained, rinsed
2 C. frozen broccoli florets, thawed
½ C. finely chopped red or green
  bell pepper

¼ C. chopped green onions
1-10¾ oz. can cream of celery soup
¾ C. skim milk
½ tsp. dried basil
1 C. crushed pretzel twists or sticks

Cook noodles to desired doneness as directed on package. Drain; keep warm. Heat oven to 350°. Spray 1½-quart casserole with non-stick cooking spray. In medium bowl, combine cooked noodles and all remaining ingredients except pretzels. Spoon mixture into spray-coated casserole; top with pretzels. Bake at 350° for 25 to 30 minutes or until thoroughly heated.

Pretzel Chicken Chunks

4 skinless, boneless chicken
  breast halves
¾ C. prepared Dijon-style mustard
2 T. honey

¼ tsp. cayenne pepper
¼ tsp. garlic salt
¾ C. crushed pretzels

Cut the skinless, boneless chicken breast halves into 1″ cubes. Preheat oven to 350°. Line a baking sheet with aluminum foil. In a small bowl, combine mustard, honey, cayenne pepper and garlic salt. Mix together and set ½ of mixture aside to be used as dipping sauce. Coat chicken chunks completely in remaining mustard mixture and then in pretzel crumbs. Place coated chicken on prepared cookie sheet. Bake in the preheated oven for 10 minutes or until golden brown. Serve with reserved mustard dip.

Pretzel Chicken

8 pieces of your favorite
 cut of chicken
1 C. pretzel crumbs
¼ C. flour
Salt and pepper to taste

Garlic powder, to taste
Paprika, to taste
½ C. soy sauce
2 T. lemon juice

Crush pretzels in blender. Mix (in a bowl or paper bag) pretzels, flour, salt, pepper, garlic powder and paprika. In another bowl, combine soy sauce and lemon juice. Dip chicken pieces in liquid mixture, then roll around (or shake in paper bag) in dry mixture. Put the coated pieces in a shallow or flat pan lined with foil. Bake in oven at 375° for 1 hour. Turn over chicken after 30 minutes.

Honey Mustard Pretzel Chicken Breasts

4 boneless, skinless chicken breasts
¾ C. Dijon mustard
¼ C. mayonnaise
2 T. honey
⅛ tsp. cayenne pepper

2 cloves garlic, minced
1 green onion, minced
Salt
Pepper
1 C. crushed pretzels

Preheat oven to 350°. Pound chicken until thin. (Easy way to pound a chicken breast: put it in a Ziploc bag first, then flatten with the mallet or whatever you're using. Keeps splatters at a minimum.) Combine mustard, mayonnaise, honey, cayenne pepper, garlic, green onions and salt and pepper to taste. Set half of mixture aside to be used as dipping sauce. Coat chicken completely in remaining mustard mixture and then dredge in pretzel crumbs. Place coated chicken on baking sheet and bake for about 30 minutes or until chicken is cooked through and juices run clear.

Strawberry Pretzel Dessert

1½ C. crushed pretzels   ¼ C. sugar
1 stick margarine, melted

Mix pretzels, margarine and sugar; press in a 9 x 13″ pan. Bake at 375° for 10 minutes.

1-8 oz. pkg. cream cheese   2-10 oz. pkgs. frozen sliced
¾ C. sugar   strawberries
2 C. whipped topping   2 C. boiling water
2-3 oz. pkgs. strawberry jello

Blend cream cheese and sugar, then beat in whipped topping and mix well. Put on top of cooled crust. Dissolve packages of jello in 2 cups of boiling water. Add frozen strawberries (do not thaw strawberries). When this starts to set, put on top of creamed mixture and refrigerate until serving time.

Variation: May use raspberries in place of strawberries.

Daiquiri Chiffon Cheesecake

CRUST:
1¼ C. crushed pretzels
½ C. white sugar

⅜ C. butter, melted

FILLING:
1-8 oz. pkg. cream cheese
1-3.5 oz. pkg. instant vanilla
  pudding mix
1½ C. milk
½ C. lime juice
1 tsp. rum flavored extract

2 tsp. grated lime zest
1 tsp. grated lemon zest
1-8 oz. container frozen whipped
  topping, thawed
Lime zest, garnish (optional)
2 limes, thinly sliced (optional)

(continued on next page)

Preheat oven to 400°.

CRUST: In a medium bowl, combine pretzel crumbs, sugar and butter. Press mixture into the bottom and 1¾" up the side of a 9" springform pan. Bake in preheated oven for about 10 minutes or until firm and lightly browned. Remove from oven and let cool completely.

FILLING: Allow cream cheese to reach room temperature. In a large bowl, beat cream cheese until smooth. In a separate bowl, combine pudding mix and milk, then mix in with cream cheese. Beat in lime juice, rum extract and lime and lemon zest. Fold ½ of the whipped topping into the mixture, then pour into cooled crust. Cover and refrigerate for at least 8 hours. Garnish with remaining whipped topping, lime zest and slices, if desired.

Lemon Pretzel Tart

½ C. white sugar
½ C. butter, softened
1½ C. crushed pretzels
1-3.5 oz. pkg. instant lemon
  pudding mix

1-8 oz. pkg. cream cheese, softened
1 C. confectioners' sugar
1-12 oz. container frozen whipped
  topping, thawed

In a mixing bowl, thoroughly cream sugar and butter. Mix in pretzels. Press mixture into a 9 x 13″ baking pan. Cover and refrigerate. Prepare lemon pudding mix according to package instructions. In a separate bowl, beat together cream cheese and confectioners' sugar. Fold in whipped topping. Spread cream cheese mixture over top of pretzel crust. Then spoon lemon pudding over cream cheese layer. Cover and refrigerate until pudding is set.

Frosty Margarita Pie

2½ C. small pretzels, finely crushed
¼ C. margarine, melted
1 T. sugar
6 C. vanilla ice cream, softened
¼ C. tequila

3 T. frozen limeade concentrate,
   thawed, but not diluted with water
1 tsp. grated lime rind
1 T. fresh lime juice
Lime slices and curls of rind, optional

Combine first three ingredients in a small bowl, stirring well. Press mixture into bottom and up sides of a 9″ pie plate. Freeze crust 1 hour. Combine ice cream and next four ingredients in a bowl, stirring well. Spoon ice cream mixture into prepared crust. Cover and freeze until firm. Let stand at room temperature 5 minutes before slicing. If desired, garnish with lime slices and lime rind curls.

Strawberry Margarita Party Pie

1½ C. crushed pretzels
¼ C. white sugar
⅔ C. butter, melted

1-14 oz. can sweetened
  condensed milk
¼ C. fresh lime juice

¼ C. tequila
4 T. orange liqueur
1 C. sliced fresh strawberries
2 drops red food coloring
2 drops yellow food coloring
2 C. whipped cream, divided

In a large bowl, combine crushed pretzels, sugar and butter. Mix well and press onto the bottom and sides of a 9″ pie pan. In a large bowl, combine sweetened condensed milk, lime juice, tequila and orange liqueur. Pour half of the mixture into another bowl. Add strawberries and a few drops of red food coloring to one half. To other half, add only a drop or two of yellow food coloring. Fold 1 cup of whipped cream into each half. Spoon into crust, alternating colors. Freeze for 4 hours or overnight.

Margarita Balls

1-12 oz. pkg. vanilla wafers
2 C. small pretzel twists
6 oz. cream cheese
1 lb. confectioners' sugar
¾ C. frozen margarita mix, thawed

2 T. tequila
2 T. Grand Marnier (orange brandy)
1 T. grated lime zest
⅔ C. white sugar
4 drops green food coloring

Using a food processor or blender, process all of the vanilla wafers and pretzels to fine crumbs. In a medium bowl, combine all of the crumbs with the confectioners' sugar. In another bowl, mix together the cream cheese, margarita mix, tequila and Grand Marnier, stir into the crumb mixture. Divide dough into two pieces, wrap and refrigerate for at least 2 hours. Divide the white sugar into two small bowls. Divide lime zest between each bowl. Stir the food coloring into one of the bowls. Unwrap dough and roll into walnut-sized balls. Roll half of the balls in the green sugar and the other half in the white sugar. Store in the refrigerator.

Chocolate Pie

1-10 oz. pkg. pretzel sticks   ¼ C. butter or margarine, melted
2 T. sugar

Crush pretzels very fine in a blender or food processor. Add sugar and butter or margarine. Mix well. Press into a 9″ pie plate. Bake at 350° for 8 minutes. Cool. Fill with Chocolate Filling.

CHOCOLATE FILLING:
⅔ C. sugar   3-3 oz. squares unsweetened
4 T. cornstarch   chocolate, broken into small pieces
2½ C. milk   3 egg yolks, slightly beaten
                                      1 tsp. vanilla extract

Combine sugar, cornstarch, milk and chocolate in the top of a double boiler. Cook over boiling water until thickened, stirring constantly. Cover and continue to cook 15 minutes. Stir part of the hot chocolate mixture into the egg yolks. Add to the remaining chocolate mixture and mix thoroughly. Cool. Add vanilla extract and mix thoroughly.

Creamy Dreamy Cherry Torte

1-14 oz. pkg. pretzels, crushed
  (about 5 C.)
½ C. butter, melted
¾ C. sugar

3 cans cherry pie filling
½ C. frozen non-dairy whipped
  topping, thawed

Crush 4 cups pretzels, save 1 cup for topping. Mix butter, sugar and pretzels together and press into a jelly roll pan. Layer cherry pie filling on top with whipped topping and remaining crushed pretzels.

Strawberry Freedom Delight

¾ C. butter or margarine, melted
¼ C. sugar
1 C. crushed pretzels
1 C. crushed tortilla chips
2 C. crushed potato chips
1-6 oz. pkg. strawberry gelatin

2 C. boiling water
2-10 oz. pkgs. frozen strawberries
1-8 oz. pkg. cream cheese
1 C. granulated sugar
2-8 oz. containers frozen non-dairy
    whipped topping, thawed

Preheat oven to 350°. Combine butter or margarine, sugar, crushed pretzels, tortilla chips and potato chips. Press into a 9 x 13″ glass dessert dish. Bake 8 minutes. Let cool. Dissolve gelatin in boiling water. Add frozen berries. Cool until gelatin begins to set. Beat cream cheese and sugar. Fold in one container of whipped topping. Spread over cooled crust. Pour strawberry gelatin mixture over cheese mixture. Spread with whipped topping.

Fourth of July Pie

1 C. crushed pretzels
½ C. butter (1 stick), melted
¼ C. sugar
2-3.4 oz. pkgs. white chocolate
  instant pudding

1¾ C. milk
2 C. sweetened whipped cream
2 C. fresh strawberries, hulled
  and sliced
2 C. fresh blueberries

In a medium bowl, combine pretzels, butter and sugar. Mix until thoroughly blended. Press mixture into the bottom of a 9″ pie plate and up the sides. In a separate bowl, mix together pudding and milk. Fold in whipped cream. Put aside 1 cup of filling for piping a garnish around the rim of the pie plate. Spread 1 cup of filling on top of pretzel crust. Layer sliced strawberries on top of filling. Cover with another layer of filling topped with blueberries. Pipe leftover filling through a star tip using a pastry bag. Chill until ready to serve.

Crispy Pretzel Bars

1 C. sugar
1 C. light corn syrup
½ C. peanut butter

5 C. crisp rice cereal
2 C. pretzel sticks
1 C. plain M&M's

In a large microwave-safe bowl, combine the sugar and corn syrup, Microwave on high for 3 minutes or until sugar is dissolved. Stir in peanut butter until blended. Add the cereal, pretzels and plain M&M's; stir until coated. Press into a greased 15 x 10 x 1″ pan. Cut into bars.

Golden Pretzel Bars

6 C. marshmallows (reserve 1 C.)
1½ C. chocolate chips
5 T. butter
¼ C. light corn syrup

1 tsp. vanilla
6 C. Golden Grahams cereal
2 C. broken pretzels

In a heavy 3-quart saucepan, melt marshmallows, chips, butter, corn syrup and vanilla over low heat. Add reserved cup of marshmallows, Golden Grahams cereal and broken pretzels. Stir until well coated. Press in a 9 x 13″ buttered pan. Cool 1 hour and cut into 24 bars.

Snack Mix Squares

2½ C. halved pretzel sticks
2 C. Corn Chex cereal
1½ C. M&M's

½ C. butter or margarine
⅓ C. creamy peanut butter
5 C. miniature marshmallows

In a large bowl, combine pretzels, cereal and M&M's. In a large saucepan over low heat, melt butter and peanut butter. Add marshmallows; cook and stir until marshmallows are melted and mixture is smooth. Pour over pretzel mixture; stir to coat. Press into greased 13 x 9 x 2″ baking pan. Cool until firm, cut into squares.

Chocolate Pretzel Bars

1½ C. crushed pretzels
½ C. (1 stick) butter, melted
1-14 oz. can chocolate-flavored
  sweetened condensed milk

1 C. (6 oz.) white chocolate chips
½ C. chopped pecans
½ C. sweetened flaked coconut

Preheat oven to 350°. Coat a 9 x 13″ baking dish with non-stick cooking spray. In a medium bowl, combine the crushed pretzels and butter, mix well and press into the bottom of the baking dish. Pour the sweetened condensed milk evenly over the pretzel mixture, then sprinkle evenly with the chips, pecans and coconut. Bake for 25 to 30 minutes or until lightly browned. Cool for 10 minutes, then chill for 30 minutes before cutting into bars and serving.

Dips, Drops & Barks

Hot Mustard Pretzel Dip

¼ C. ground mustard
¼ C. vinegar
¼ C. sugar

1 egg yolk
2 T. honey
Pretzels for dipping

In a small pan, combine mustard and vinegar; let stand 30 minutes. Whisk in the sugar and egg yolk until smooth. Cook over medium heat, whisking constantly until mixture begins to simmer and is thickened (about 7 minutes). Remove from heat. Whisk in honey. Chill. Serve with pretzels.

White Chocolate Pretzels

1-12 oz. pkg. white chocolate   1-9 oz. pkg. small pretzels

Slowly melt white chocolate in an appropriate pan or follow directions on package. Dip pretzels in white chocolate and lay on wax paper to firm. When firm, may put in a covered bowl or in a bag.

Peanut Butterscotch Pretzel Rods

1-11 oz. pkg. butterscotch chips	About 60 (3″) twisted pretzels
⅓ C. creamy peanut butter	2 to 3 T. sesame seeds, toasted

In a medium microwave-safe bowl on medium-high power, microwave butterscotch chips and peanut butter for 1 minute; stir. Microwave at additional 10 to 20 second intervals, stirring until smooth. Dip about ¾ of one pretzel in butterscotch mixture; shake off excess. Place on wire rack; sprinkle lightly with sesame seeds. Repeat with remaining pretzels. Refrigerate for 20 minutes or until set.

Peppermint Pretzel Dippers

2 C. (12 oz.) semi-sweet
   chocolate chips
1 T. shortening (or butter)

1-10 oz. pkg. pretzel rods
40 red and/or green hard mint
   candies, crushed

Place chocolate chips and shortening in a 2-cup microwave-safe measuring cup. Heat until melted. Stir until smooth. Break each pretzel rod in half. Dip the broken end about halfway into melted chocolate. Roll in crushed candies. Place on a waxed paper-lined baking sheet. Chill until set.

Pretzel Sparklers

24 long rod pretzels
2 C. white chocolate or almond bark, melted

1 C. sprinkles, star cake decorations or mini M&M's

Dip the pretzel rod halfway into the melted white chocolate or almond bark, then sprinkle with sprinkles, cake decorations or mini M&M's over the wet chocolate. Lay on wax paper or place in a cup to dry.

Chocolate-Caramel Dipped Pretzel Rods

2-14 oz. pkgs. caramels
2-10 oz. pkgs. pretzel rods
3 C. chopped toasted almonds

1 lb. vanilla almond bark
1 lb. chocolate almond bark

Melt caramels in the top of a double boiler or microwave-safe bowl. Pour into an ungreased 8″ square pan. Leaving 1″ of space on the end you are holding, roll or dip pretzels in caramel. Allow excess to drip off. Roll in almonds. Place on waxed paper-lined baking sheets and allow to harden. Melt vanilla almond bark in a double boiler or microwave. Repeat dipping procedure with half of the caramel-coated pretzels. Return to baking sheets to harden. Repeat with chocolate almond bark and remaining pretzels. Store in airtight container or wrap in plastic wrap and tie with a colored ribbon for gift giving.

Candy-Dipped Pretzels

6 C. candy melts in assorted colors   Assorted sprinkles or candy decors
12 large pretzel twists   Candy gift bags and ribbon, optional

Line several baking sheets with wax paper. Melt candy melts, one color at a time, according to package directions. Dip half of each pretzel into candy melt allowing excess to drip off. Place on wax paper; lightly sprinkle with sprinkles. Set aside until set, at least 30 minutes. If desired, place pretzels in bags; tie with ribbon.

Turtzels

2 bags vanilla caramels
1 C. chopped pecans
1-10 oz. pkg. pretzel rods

Chocolate almond bark
Vanilla almond bark

Melt caramels in microwave-safe dish. Coat ¾ of one pretzel rod in melted caramel; roll in chopped pecans. Allow to cool and firm up on chilled waxed paper-lined baking sheets, turning as necessary to keep rounded shape. Melt chocolate almond bark in microwave-safe bowl. Coat caramel coated pretzel rods; cool and chill on baking sheets again. Drizzle melted vanilla almond bark over pretzel to complete.

Candy Stacks

4 C. cereal (your favorite kind)   1 C. macadamia nuts, chopped
2 C. pretzels, broken   1 lb. white candy coating

In a large bowl, mix cereal, broken pretzels and nuts. In a microwave-safe bowl, melt white candy coating. Pour over cereal mixture and mix well. Drop by spoonfuls onto waxed paper-lined cookie sheets. Chill in refrigerator until set.

Sweet Pretzel Stacks

2 C. crushed pretzels
¼ C. peanuts
⅔ C. sweetened condensed milk

½ C. semi-sweet chocolate chips
½ C. butterscotch chips
¼ tsp. vanilla extract

In a large mixing bowl, combine pretzels and peanuts. Set aside. In a medium saucepan, mix together condensed milk, chocolate chips and butterscotch chips. Cook over low heat stirring constantly until chips are melted (about 5 minutes). Remove pan from heat and stir in vanilla extract. Pour saucepan mixture over the pretzel/peanut mixture and stir until thoroughly coated. Drop by rounded teaspoons onto waxed paper or foil. Cool (or chill) until firm. Store in covered container in cool place (or in refrigerator).

Crunchy Pretzel Drops

6 oz. butterscotch chips
¼ C. light corn syrup
2 T. milk
2 T. butter

1 tsp. vanilla
3½ C. puffed corn cereal
1 C. broken pretzels

Mix first five ingredients in saucepan. Melt over low heat, stirring constantly. Remove from heat and stir in cereal and pretzels. Drop by rounded tablespoonfuls onto wax paper and allow to harden.

Chocolate Pretzel Kisses

Miniature pretzels   M&M's
Hershey's Kisses

Arrange miniature pretzels on ungreased cookie tray. Place unwrapped Hershey's Kiss on top of each pretzel. Put tray in a preheated oven at 250° for 5 minutes. Take out and immediately push an M&M into top of softened Kiss and allow to cool.

Chocolate-Caramel Pretzels

Mini pretzels (round)   M&M's
Rolos

Place pretzels on greased baking sheets. Place Rolos in center of each pretzel. Bake at 275° for 2 to 3 minutes. Remove from oven. Place M&M's on each and press down lightly so that chocolate and caramel (Rolos) fills the pretzel. Refrigerate until chocolate is firm. Store at room temperature.

Pretzel Cookies

2 lbs. white chocolate bark
  (can be melted in microwave
  or double boiler)
8″ to 10″ long stick pretzels, broken
  into thirds

2 C. Rice Krispies and 2 C. Captain
  Crunch (or 4 C. Rice Krispies)
1 C. Spanish peanuts (or any other
  type of nut)

Mix pretzels, cereal and peanuts together. Pour melted bark over all and spoon out on wax paper to form candy. Candy will harden as it dries.

Festive Holiday Bark

16 oz. vanilla flavored confectioners'
  coating

2 C. small pretzel twists
½ C. M&M's

Line a cookie sheet with waxed paper. Place candy coating in a microwave safe bowl. Microwave for 2½ minutes. Stir and microwave at 30-second intervals until completely melted and smooth. Place pretzels and candy coated chocolate pieces in a large bowl. Pour melted coating over and stir until well coated. Spread onto waxed paper lined baking sheet. Let stand until firm or place in refrigerator to set up faster.

Sticks and Stones Candy Bark

1-11 oz. pkg. butterscotch flavored
  chips, divided
1½ C. semi-sweet chocolate chips
½ C. creamy peanut butter

2 C. thin pretzel sticks
2 C. dry roasted peanuts
1-10 oz. pkg. semi-sweet chocolate
  covered raisins

Butter a 9 x 13″ glass baking dish. Microwave 1⅓ cups butterscotch chips, semi-sweet chips and peanut butter in large microwave-safe bowl on high (100%) power for 1 minute; stir. Microwave at additional 10 to 20-second intervals, stirring until smooth. Add pretzels, peanuts and chocolate covered raisins; stir well to coat. Spread into prepared baking dish. Place remaining butterscotch chips in small, heavy-duty plastic bag. Microwave on medium-high (70%) power for 30 seconds; knead bag to mix. Microwave at additional 10 to 20-second intervals, kneading until smooth. Cut tiny corner from bag; squeeze to drizzle over candy. Refrigerate for 1 hour or until firm. Break into bite-size pieces.

White Chocolate Mix

2 lbs. white chocolate
6 C. crispy rice cereal squares
3 C. toasted oat cereal

2 C. thin pretzel sticks
2 C. cashews
1-12 oz. pkg. mini candy-coated
   chocolate pieces

Melt chocolate in a large saucepan over low heat or in microwave until just soft. Stir until melted. Combine all the other ingredients in a big roasting pan or bowl. Stir chocolate into mixture. Turn out on waxed paper. Combine the crispy rice cereal squares, toasted oat cereal, pretzels, cashews and candy in a big roaster pan or bowl. Stir chocolate into mixture. Turn out on waxed paper and let cool.

Peanut & Pretzel Bark

1-28 oz. pkg. chocolate or vanilla   1½ C. broken thin pretzels
  flavored candy coating   1 C. coarsely chopped peanuts

In heavy saucepan over low heat, melt candy coating, stirring frequently. Remove from heat; stir in remaining ingredients. Spread into thin layer on two aluminum foil-lined baking sheets. Chill 30 minutes or until firm. Break into chunks. Store covered at room temperature or in refrigerator.

Sweet Crunchies

Butterscotch Cereal Toss

1 C. salted peanuts
2 C. pretzel sticks
2 qts. cereal: Cheerios, Rice Chex,
  Corn Chex, Wheat Chex, etc.
½ C. butter

¼ C. light corn syrup
1½ C. brown sugar
½ tsp. salt
1 tsp. vanilla

Mix peanuts, pretzels and cereal together in a large bowl. Put butter, corn syrup, sugar and salt in a saucepan, bring to a boil over medium heat, then boil for 2 minutes. Add vanilla. Mix and pour over cereal mixture. Toss until coated. Put waxed paper on countertop and spread mixture over it. Cool and let dry for 6 to 8 hours. Break apart and store in tight container.

You may also cool this in the freezer.

Caramel Pretzels and Nuts

16 C. small pretzels
2 C. roasted peanuts
Vegetable cooking spray
2 C. firmly packed brown sugar
¼ C. light corn syrup

¼ C. molasses
1 tsp. salt
1 tsp. baking soda
1 tsp. almond extract

Place pretzels and peanuts in a 14 x 20″ oven cooking bag sprayed with cooking spray. In a 2-quart microwave-safe bowl, combine brown sugar, corn syrup and molasses. Microwave on high power for 2 minutes or until mixture boils. Stir and microwave 2 minutes longer. Stir in salt, baking soda and almond extract. Pour syrup over pretzel mixture. Stir and shake bag until well coated. Microwave 1½ minutes on high. Stir and shake. Microwave 1½ minutes longer. Spread on greased aluminum foil, cool completely. Store in airtight container.

Sweet Pretzel Crunch

4 C. pretzel sticks or pretzel twists   2-10 oz. bags white chocolate chips
1 can sweetened condensed milk   1 C. dried fruit, optional

Line 15 x 10" baking pan with aluminum foil. In a large saucepan, heat condensed milk over low heat 5 minutes. Remove from burner; stir in white chips until melted and well mixed. Pour mixture over pretzels, coating well. Right away, spread mixture into prepared pan. Sprinkle the dried fruit; lightly press down on mixture. Refrigerate for 1 to 2 hours. Break into pieces and gobble up.

Caramel Corn Snack Mix

1 C. unpopped popcorn	1 tsp. baking powder
2 T. vegetable oil	½ tsp. vanilla extract
½ C. butter or margarine	2 C. small pretzel twists
1 C. packed brown sugar	4 C. crispy rice cereal squares
½ C. light corn syrup	2 C. pecan halves

Preheat oven to 250°. Place popcorn in a large pot with 2 tablespoons vegetable oil. Over a low heat, begin to pop the popcorn. Constantly shake the pot to ensure that the popcorn kernels and oil do not burn. Once the popping has slowed, remove the pot from heat. In a large saucepan, mix butter or margarine, brown sugar and corn syrup. Bring this mixture to a boil (over a medium heat) while stirring constantly. Reduce heat to medium-low and do not stir for 5 minutes. Remove the pan from heat and mix in baking powder and vanilla extract, stirring carefully. In a large baking pan, combine popcorn, pretzels, cereal and pecans. Pour the butter mixture over the popcorn mixture, stir to coat. Bake for 30 minutes, stirring the mixture after the first 15 minutes have elapsed.

Snicky Snackies

15 oz. mini twist pretzels
2 C. mixed nuts
1 C. unsalted butter

2 C. packed dark brown sugar
½ C. light corn syrup
Pinch of salt

Preheat oven to 250°. In a 9 x 13˝ baking dish, combine the pretzels and nuts, set aside. In a large saucepan, combine the butter, sugar, corn syrup and salt. Stir together over medium heat until sugar dissolves. Bring to a boil and cook until very thick and at the "firm ball" stage (260° F.). Remove from heat, pour over pretzel/nut mixture and mix all together. Bake in the preheated oven for 20 minutes, stirring after 10 minutes. Remove from oven and spread out on wax paper to cool.

Nutty Snack Mix

1-12 oz. box Crispix cereal
1 C. peanuts
1 C. walnuts

1 C. pecans
1-6 oz. pkg. pretzel sticks

Mix together well. In large kettle combine:

2 C. brown sugar
1 C. butter

½ C. light corn syrup
1 tsp. salt

Bring to a good boil, stirring constantly. Add 1 teaspoon baking soda (will foam). Pour over cereal mix; mix well. Microwave for 6 minutes in a brown paper bag, stirring every 2 minutes.

Sweet Chex Mix

½ C. margarine
1 C. brown sugar
½ C. light corn syrup
1½ C. pretzels

1½ C. peanuts
1½ C. Cheerios cereal
3 C. Chex cereal

Boil margarine, brown sugar and syrup for 2 minutes. Quickly pour mixture over the pretzels, peanuts, Cheerios and Chex that have been mixed together. Mix well and toss into a large brown paper bag. Microwave ½ minute; shake. Microwave 1½ minutes; shake. Microwave 2 minutes. Spread on cookie sheet to cool.

Honey-Glazed Snack Mix

4 C. rice, corn or wheat cereal   ⅓ C. margarine
1½ C. mini-pretzels   ¼ C. honey
1 C. mixed nuts

Combine cereal, pretzels, and nuts in large bowl. Melt margarine in saucepan. Stir in honey. Pour over cereal mixture; toss to coat. Spread in 10 x 15″ baking pan. Bake at 350° for 12 to 15 minutes, stirring occasionally. Cool slightly. Spread on waxed paper to cool completely.

Critter Crunch

¼ C. butter or margarine
3 T. brown sugar
1 tsp. ground cinnamon
1½ C. Crispix cereal
1½ C. Cheerios cereal

1½ C. animal crackers
1½ C. bear-shaped honey
   graham snacks
1 C. bite-size shredded wheat
1 C. miniature pretzels

In a saucepan or microwave-safe bowl, heat butter, brown sugar and cinnamon until butter is melted; mix well. In a large bowl, combine the remaining ingredients. Add butter mixture and toss to coat. Place in a greased 15 x 10 x 1″ baking pan. Bake uncovered at 300° for 30 minutes, stirring every 10 minutes. Store in airtight container.

Halloween Party Mix

1-11 oz. pkg. pretzels
1-10 to 12-oz. pkg. peanut butter
filled butter-flavored crackers
(miniatures)
1 C. dry roasted peanuts
1 C. sugar

½ C. butter or margarine
½ C. light corn syrup
2 T. vanilla
1 tsp. baking soda
1-10 oz. pkg. M&M's
1-18½ oz. pkg. candy corn

In a large bowl, combine pretzels, crackers and peanuts. In a large saucepan, combine sugar, butter and corn syrup. Bring to a boil over medium heat; boil 5 minutes. Remove from heat; stir in vanilla and soda (mixture will foam). Pour over pretzel mixture; stir until coated. Pour into a greased 15 x 10 x 1″ pan. Bake at 250° for 45 minutes, stirring every 15 minutes. Break apart while warm. Toss with M&M's and candy corn. Cool completely. Store in airtight container.

White Chocolate Party Mix

1-10 oz. pkg. mini-pretzels
5 C. Corn Chex
1 lb. M&M's
5 C. Cheerios

2 C. salted peanuts
2-12 oz. pkgs. vanilla chips
3 T. vegetable oil

In large bowl, combine first five ingredients, set aside. In microwave-safe bowl, heat vanilla chips and oil on medium-high (approximately 2 minutes), stirring once. Stir until smooth. Pour over cereal mixture and mix well. Spread onto 3 wax paper-lined baking sheets. Cool, then break apart. Store in airtight containers.

Cinnamon Snack Mix

11 whole cinnamon graham crackers,
  broken into bite-size pieces
1-17.9 oz. pkg. Crispix cereal
1 C. miniature pretzels

1 C. pecan halves
⅔ C. butter or margarine, melted
1/2 C. honey
1 C. vanilla or butterscotch chips

In a large bowl, combine graham crackers, cereal, pretzels and pecans. Combine butter and honey. Drizzle over graham cracker mixture and mix well. Transfer to two greased 15 x 10 x 1" baking pans. Bake at 350° for 12 to 15 minutes, stirring once. Cool completely. Stir in chips.

Pretzel Party Mix

2 C. toasted cereal squares
2 C. small pretzel twists
1 C. dry roasted peanuts
1 C. (about 20) caramels, unwrapped
   and coarsely chopped

1⅔ to 2 C. (11 to 12 oz. pkg.) milk
   chocolate, butterscotch flavored
   or white morsels

Coat 9 x 13″ baking pan with non-stick cooking spray. Combine cereal, pretzels, peanuts and caramels in large bowl. Microwave morsels in medium microwave-safe bowl on medium-high (70%) power (100% power for semi-sweet chocolate morsels) for 1 minute: stir. Microwave at additional 10 to 20-second intervals, stirring until smooth. Pour over cereal mixture; stir to coat evenly. Spread mixture in prepared baking pan; cool for 30 to 45 minutes or until firm. Break into bite-size pieces.

Reindeer Munchies

5 C. sweetened corn and oat
  honeycomb-shaped cereal or
  cereal squares
2 C. thin pretzel sticks, broken in half
½ C. butter
½ C. creamy peanut butter

1-11.5 oz. pkg. (1½ C.) real milk
  chocolate chips
1 C. powdered sugar
1 C. red and green candy-coated
  milk chocolate candies

Mix cereal and pretzels in 4-quart bowl; set aside. Place butter, peanut butter and chocolate chips in medium microwave-safe bowl. Microwave on high for 45 seconds; stir. Continue microwaving until butter and chocolate are melted (15 to 45 seconds). Stir until smooth. Immediately pour chocolate mixture over cereal in bowl; stir until well coated. Spread mixture evenly into single layer on two waxed paper-lined baking sheets. Refrigerate 20 minutes to set. Break into bite-sized pieces; place half of mixture in each plastic food bag. Pour ½ cup powdered sugar into each bag; seal bags. Shake bags until mixture is well coated. Place ½ cup candies in each bag. Seal bags; gently shake bags to distribute candies. Store mixture in sealed bags or airtight container in refrigerator up to 4 weeks.

Molasses Munchies

16 C. miniature pretzels
2 C. roasted peanuts
Vegetable cooking spray
2 C. firmly packed brown sugar
¼ C. light corn syrup

¼ C. molasses
1 tsp. salt
1 tsp. baking soda
1 tsp. almond extract

Place pretzels and peanuts in a 14 x 20″ oven cooking bag coated with cooking spray. In a 2-quart microwave-safe bowl, combine brown sugar, corn syrup and molasses. Microwave on high for 2 minutes or until mixture boils. Stir and microwave 2 minutes longer. Stir in salt, baking soda and almond extract and pour over pretzel mixture in bag. Shake until well coated, microwave 1½ minutes, shake and microwave 1½ minutes longer. Spread on greased aluminum foil; cool completely. Store in airtight container.

Spicy Munchies

Nuts and Bolts

1 C. corn oil
1 medium bag thin pretzels
1 can salted peanuts
1 can salted mixed nuts

1 small box each Rice Chex,
  Wheat Chex, Corn Chex
¼ C. Worcestershire sauce
¼ C. onion salt
¼ C. garlic salt

Mix sauce and spices in oil. In a large, shallow roasting pan, layer cereal (mixed), pretzels and nuts, drizzling each layer with the oil mixture. Bake at 250° for 2 hours, stirring every half hour.

Ranch Pretzels

2 lbs. Bavarian pretzels or sourdough
    hard pretzels (the big fat ones)
2 lbs. pretzels
1 pkg. ranch dressing mix (dry powder)

1 C. vegetable oil
½ tsp. lemon pepper
½ tsp. garlic powder
½ tsp. dill weed

Break or smash pretzels into bite-sized pieces. Pour pretzels into baking pans. (You will probably need 2 rectangular cake pans.) Mix all other ingredients together and pour over pretzels. Stir to make sure they are completely coated. Leave sit for about an hour allowing flavors to soak in and then preheat oven to 350°. Bake for about 20 minutes, stirring once or twice. Allow to cool and store in airtight containers.

No-Bake Party Mix

8 C. Crispix cereal
2½ C. mini-pretzel sticks
2½ C. mini Cheddar cheese crackers

3 T. vegetable oil
1 env. ranch salad dressing mix

In a heavy 2-gallon bag, combine cereal, pretzels and crackers; drizzle with oil. Seal and gently toss. Sprinkle with dressing mix. Seal and toss again. Store in an airtight container.

Ranch Snack Mix

1-12 oz. pkg. mini pretzels
2-6 oz. pkgs. Bugles
1-10 oz. can salted cashews

1-6 oz. pkg. bite-size Cheddar
   cheese fish crackers
1 env. ranch salad dressing mix
¾ C. vegetable oil

In two large bowls, combine the pretzels, Bugles, cashews and crackers. Sprinkle with dressing mix; toss gently to combine. Drizzle with oil; toss until well coated. Store in airtight containers.

Taco Snack Mix

4 C. spoon-size shredded wheat
4 C. pretzel sticks
4 C. tortilla chips

1¼ oz. pkg. taco seasoning mix
¼ C. margarine, melted

In large bowl, combine cereal, pretzels, tortilla chips and taco seasoning mix. Drizzle with margarine, tossing to coat well. Store in airtight container.

Taco Munch

6 oz. can French fried onions
4 C. Crispix cereal
8 oz. can potato sticks
1 pkg. taco seasoning

2 C. peanuts
½ C. butter, melted
4 C. pretzels

Mix ingredients together except butter and seasoning. Pour butter and seasoning over other ingredients and stir until well coated. Bake at 200° for 1 hour. Stir every 15 minutes.

Texas Trash

¾ C. bacon grease (or margarine)
1½ sticks margarine
3 T. Worcestershire sauce
3 T. garlic salt
1½ tsp. Accent (or MSG)
2 T. Tabasco sauce

1 large can mixed nuts
½ box Cheerios
2 boxes pretzels
½ box Wheat Chex
½ box Rice Chex
Oyster crackers, optional

Melt first six ingredients in saucepan and pour over the next six ingredients. Bake 1½ hours at 225°. Stir every 15 minutes. Place in coffee cans or covered containers and serve for snacks.

73

Crunchy Italian Mix

½ C. butter or margarine
1 T. Worcestershire sauce
1 tsp. Italian seasoning
½ tsp. garlic powder
5 C. Crispix cereal

2 C. Cheerios cereal
2½ C. mini pretzels
1-10 oz. can mixed nuts
¼ C. grated Parmesan cheese

In a saucepan or microwave-safe bowl, heat the first four ingredients until butter is melted. Mix well. In a large bowl, combine the cereals, pretzels, nuts and Parmesan cheese. Drizzle with butter mixture and mix well. Place in an ungreased 15 x 10 x 1″ baking pan. Bake uncovered at 250° for 45 minutes, stirring every 15 minutes.

Creole Party Mix

½ lb. cashews
½ lb. hot roasted peanuts
2 C. pretzel nuggets
8 C. waffle cereal (such as Chex)

1 C. butter
½ C. Worcestershire sauce
2 T. Creole spice

Preheat oven to 325°. In a large bowl, combine nuts, pretzels and cereal. Melt butter with Worcestershire sauce and drizzle over nut mixture; sprinkle with Creole spice. Toss to coat completely, pour onto a cookie sheet and bake until crisp and tasty, about 25 minutes.

Buttery Onion Pretzels

1¼ C. butter or margarine   1-16 oz. bag chunky pretzels
1-1½ oz. pkg. dry onion soup mix

In a skillet, melt butter. Stir in soup mix. Heat and stir until well mixed. Add pretzels; toss to coat. Spread pretzel mixture in a baking pan. Bake at 250° for 1½ hours, stirring every 15 minutes. Cool. Store in an airtight container.

Oyster Cracker Snacks

1-12 oz. pkg. oyster crackers   ½ tsp. garlic salt
1-5 oz. pkg. pretzel sticks   1 pkg. ranch dressing mix, dry
1 T. dill weed

Shake all this up in a bag and add ¾ to 1 cup of vegetable oil; shake some more.
Ready to eat for snacks or in soups or salads.

Slow Cooker Party Mix

4 C. Wheat Chex
4 C. Cheerios
3 C. pretzel sticks
1-12 oz. can salted peanuts

¼ C. butter, melted
2 to 3 T. grated Parmesan cheese
1 tsp. celery salt
½ to ¾ tsp. seasoned salt

In a 5-quart slow cooker, mix cereals, pretzels and peanuts. In a small bowl, combine butter, Parmesan cheese, celery salt and seasoned salt; drizzle over cereal mixture and mix well. Cover and cook on low for up to 3 hours, stirring every 30 minutes. Serve warm.

Peppery Pretzels

1 tsp. ground cayenne pepper	1-1 oz. pkg. dry ranch dressing mix
1 tsp. lemon pepper	¾ C. vegetable oil
1½ tsp. garlic salt	1½-15 oz. pkgs. mini-pretzels

In a small bowl, mix together cayenne pepper, lemon pepper, garlic salt, ranch dressing mix and vegetable oil. Place pretzels in a large, sealable plastic bag. Pour in mixture from bowl. Shake well. Allow pretzels to marinate in the mixture approximately 2 hours before serving. Shake occasionally to maintain coating.

Cheddar-Ranch Snack Mix

5 C. white Cheddar baked
  snack crackers
2 C. mini pretzel braids
2 C. crispy cereal squares
½ C. vegetable oil

½ tsp. lemon and herb seasoning
¼ tsp. garlic powder
¼ tsp. dill weed
1-1 oz. pkg. ranch style dip mix

Mix white Cheddar crackers, pretzels and cereal squares in a large microwavable bowl. In a separate bowl, combine remaining ingredients. Pour seasoning mixture over the crackers, pretzels and cereal squares and blend well. Microwave on high for 1 minute. Dry on paper towels and store in an airtight container.

Garlic Pretzels

1-20 oz. bag broken pretzels
1 env. onion soup mix
2 T. Worcestershire sauce

2 tsp. garlic powder
1 C. (2 sticks) butter, melted

Place pretzels in a large baking pan with sides. In a small mixing bowl, combine soup mix, Worcestershire, garlic powder and melted butter, stirring until well blended. Pour over pretzels. Bake at 250° for 1 hour, stirring often.

81

Ranch Mini Pretzels

½ C. (1 stick) butter, melted
1 env. ranch dressing mix
1 T. Worcestershire sauce

½ tsp. seasoned salt
Dash of hot sauce
7 to 8 C. mini pretzels

Mix all ingredients except pretzels. Toss with pretzels and place in a large baking dish or roaster. Bake for 1 hour at 250°, stirring every 15 minutes.

Hook, Line 'n Sinker Mix

3 T. butter or margarine, melted
1 T. dried parsley flakes
¾ tsp. dried tarragon
½ tsp. onion powder
¼ to ½ tsp. celery salt

1 C. goldfish crackers
1 C. pretzel sticks
½ C. Cheerios
½ C. dry roasted peanuts

In a 2-quart microwave-safe bowl, combine the first five ingredients; mix well. Add crackers, pretzels, Cheerios and peanuts; toss to coat. Microwave, uncovered on high for 1½ minutes, stirring once. Cool completely. Store in an airtight container.

Zesty Snack Mix

11 C. Cheerios
8 C. Crispix
8 C. Corn Chex
6 C. bite-size shredded wheat
1-10 oz. pkg. corn chips
1-8 oz. jar salted peanuts
1-8 oz. pkg. pretzel sticks
1-7 oz. pkg. shoestring potato sticks

1-7 oz. pkg. sesame sticks
1 lb. butter or margarine
3 T. garlic powder
3 T. onion powder
2 T. hot pepper sauce
2 T. lemon juice
2 T. Worcestershire sauce
2 tsp. garlic salt

In large bowl, combine the first nine ingredients. In a saucepan over low heat, melt butter. Add seasonings; stir until dissolved. Pour over cereal mixture; stir to coat. Place in large greased roasting pans. Bake, uncovered, at 250° for 1 hour, stirring every 15 minutes. Store in airtight containers.

Sideliner's Snack

6 qts. popped popcorn
4 C. corn chips
2 C. stick pretzels
1-4 oz. can diced green chilies

½ C. melted butter
1½ tsp. seasoning salt
2 C. shredded Cheddar cheese

In large shallow baking pans, combine popped corn, corn chips, pretzels, chilies, butter and salt; toss gently. Sprinkle with cheese. Bake at 350° for 10 minutes or until cheese melts. Serve warm.

Glazed Honey Mustard Pretzels

12 C. miniature pretzel twists
2 T. margarine (not low-fat)
2 T. yellow mustard

¼ C. honey
½ tsp. garlic salt
½ tsp. onion powder

Preheat oven to 250°. Spray a large roasting pan with non-stick cooking spray and put pretzels in it. Combine margarine, mustard, honey, garlic salt and onion powder. Microwave or heat on stove until hot. Drizzle over pretzels while stirring carefully to coat well. Bake for 1 hour, stirring every 15 minutes. Pour out onto waxed paper and quickly separate into a single layer. Cool completely. Store in sealed bag or container.

Snack Attack Party Mix

½ C. margarine
1 tsp. garlic salt
4 T. Worcestershire sauce
3 C. mini-pretzels

2 C. peanuts
6 C. popped popcorn
2 C. corn nuts

Preheat oven to 250°. Melt margarine in saucepan and remove from heat. Add garlic salt and Worcestershire sauce. Mix snacks together and coat with margarine mixture. Place in shallow baking pan and bake for 45 minutes, stirring occasionally. Cool completely before serving.

Spicy Nut & Raisin Mix

2 T. peanut oil
2 cloves garlic, crushed
⅔ C. unblanched almonds
⅔ C. pine nuts
⅔ C. unsalted cashews
2 tsp. Worcestershire sauce

2 tsp. chili powder
1 tsp. cayenne
1⅓ C. thin pretzel sticks, broken
  in 1″ pieces
1 C. raisins
1 tsp. salt

In a large cast iron skillet, over a medium heat, warm the oil. Add the garlic and cook 1 to 2 minutes. Add the almonds, pine nuts and cashews. Add the Worcestershire sauce, chili powder and cayenne. Mix well. Stir in the pretzels and cook 3 to 4 minutes, stirring constantly. Remove from the heat. Add the raisins and salt. Mix well. Turn the mixture into a serving dish and cool.

Southwestern Snack Mix

4 C. popped popcorn
3 C. miniature pretzel twists
2 C. miniature garlic flavored bagel chips
1 C. corn chips
3 T. margarine or butter, melted
1 tsp. paprika

¾ tsp. chili powder
½ tsp. cumin
¼ tsp. onion powder
¼ tsp. garlic powder
Dash of ground red pepper (cayenne)

In a large bowl, combine popcorn, pretzels, bagel chips and corn chips. In a small bowl, combine all remaining ingredients; mix well. Pour evenly over popcorn mixture; toss gently to coat. Store in tightly covered container.

Edible Art

Reindeer Cookies

1 pkg. refrigerated peanut butter
  cookie dough
1 pkg. small pretzel twists

1 pkg. mini chocolate chips
1 pkg. red hots

Freeze cookie dough for 15 minutes. Keep in freezer between batches. Cut dough into ¼″ slices and place about 4″ apart on a cookie sheet. Pinch in each side about ⅔'s of the way down to make face. Place pretzel twists into top for antlers and chocolate chips for eyes. Bake at 350° for about 10 minutes. Remove from oven and press red hot in for nose.

Snowshoe Cookies

12 Nutter Butter cookies
⅓ C. semi-sweet chocolate chips,
  melted

12 miniature marshmallows
12 pretzel sticks

Place cookies on a wire rack over a large piece of waxed paper. Drizzle chocolate over cookies in a crisscross pattern to form showshoes. Let stand until chocolate has hardened. For ski poles, thread a marshmallow on one end of each pretzel stick. Serve a set of poles with a pair of snowshoes.

Spider Web Apples

10 medium apples
10 wooden craft sticks
2-14 oz. pkgs. caramels
⅓ C. water
2½ C. coarsely crushed, salted
  thin pretzel sticks

1-16 oz. container ready-to-spread
  chocolate frosting
1-16 oz. container ready-to-spread
  vanilla frosting

(continued on next page)

Wash and dry apples. Remove stems and insert wooden craft sticks into stem ends of apples. Set aside. Cook caramels and ⅓ cup water in a large saucepan over low to medium heat until smooth, stirring frequently. Remove from heat. Dip apples into hot caramel, spooning caramel mixture over apples to coat completely. Scrape excess caramel from bottom of each apple; roll coated apples in crushed pretzels and place on greased wax paper-lined baking sheet. Refrigerate at least 15 minutes or until caramel is set. Spoon chocolate frosting into a small heavy-duty zip-top plastic bag; seal bag. Submerge bag in a small saucepan of hot water until frosting is thin enough to pipe. Snip a tiny hole in one corner of bag, using scissors. Drizzle warm chocolate in a webbed design over each apple. Repeat heating and drizzling procedure with vanilla frosting. Chill apples until firm. Wrap apples in cellophane wrap and tie with heavy string.

Fried Egg Candy

1 pkg. pretzel sticks   Yellow plain M&M's
1-12 oz. white chocolate chips

Place pretzel sticks on wax paper in groups of two. Leave a small space between each. In microwave, heat chips at 70% power until melted. Stir until smooth. Drop by spoonfuls over pretzel sticks. For the yolks, place one or two M&M's in the center of the egg.

Chocolate Peanut Butter Frogs

2-1 oz. squares semi-sweet baking
  chocolate
2 T. butter or margarine
12 chocolate sandwich cookies

3 T. creamy peanut butter
24 miniature pretzel twists
24 M&M's

Place chocolate and butter in saucepan; cook over low heat until melted, stirring frequently. Set aside. Spread bottom of each cookie with 1 teaspoon of peanut butter; dip into melted chocolate mixture. Immediately press 2 pretzel twists on chocolate for frog legs with wide part of pretzels facing outward. Place pretzel-size down, on wax paper-lined cookie sheet. Attach M&M's for eyes using remaining chocolate mixture or peanut butter. Let stand until chocolate is set.

Angel Cookies

1-8 oz. pkg. refrigerated sugar
  cookie dough
72 small pretzel twists

Decorator sugar or regular sugar
Vanilla frosting

Preheat the oven to 350°. For easier slicing and shaping, work with half roll of well-chilled dough at a time; refrigerate remaining dough until needed. Slice dough into ¼″ slices. For each angel, cut narrow strip from 2 sides of slice, forming a triangle. Roll strips into 1 ball. Place triangle on ungreased cookie sheet. To form wings, place 2 pretzels on either side of top point of triangle, making sure single hole side of pretzels touches dough. Place ball on top of triangle to form head; press with fingers to flatten. Repeat with remaining dough slices and pretzels, placing 2″ apart on cookie sheets. Sprinkle with sugar. Bake 7 to 11 minutes or until golden brown. Cool for 1 minute; remove from cookie sheets. Pipe vanilla frosting around outside edges of cookie and around pretzel twists. Pipe on hair and continue to decorate as desired.

Rudolph Cupcakes

24 paper baking cups
1 pkg. cake mix, any flavor
1-16 oz. tub chocolate frosting
Chocolate sprinkles

24 large pretzel twists
24 miniature marshmallows
24 red cinnamon candies
24 small red gumdrops

Prepare and bake cake mix according to package directions for cupcakes. Cool completely. Frost cupcakes with frosting. Sprinkle chocolate sprinkles over tops of cupcakes. For each cupcake, cut pretzel twist in half; arrange on cupcake for reindeer antlers. Cut miniature marshmallow in half; arrange on cupcake for eyes. Center gumdrop below marshmallow halves for nose. Place red cinnamon candy below gumdrop for mouth. Store loosely covered.

Snowman Crispies

3 T. butter or margarine
1-10 oz. pkg. marshmallows
6 C. crispy rice cereal
5 round red peppermint candies
8 red jelly beans

10 chocolate chips
25 miniature chocolate chips
1 fruit roll up, cut into ¾″ strips
15 red cinnamon candies
10 pretzel sticks

Line a baking sheet with wax paper and coat with non-stick cooking spray. In a microwave safe bowl, heat butter and marshmallows on high for 2 to 3 minutes, stirring at the halfway point. Stir until smooth. Add crispy rice cereal. Stir until well coated. Using a ¾ cup portion of the mixture for each, form 5 balls and place on the baking sheet. Using a ⅓ cup portion for each, form 5 more balls. Place the smaller balls on top of the larger ones, forming snowmen. Decorate by placing 1 jelly bean on 1 peppermint candy for the hat; place on top of smaller ball. Slice a jelly bean in 1/2 lengthwise for the nose, 2 chocolate chips make the eyes and 5 mini chips make the mouth. A strip of fruit roll up adds a scarf, 3 red cinnamon candies for buttons and 2 pretzel sticks make the arms.

Witches' Brooms

½ C. brown sugar
½ C. butter or margarine, softened
2 T. water
1 tsp. vanilla
1½ C. all-purpose flour
⅛ tsp. salt

10 pretzel rods, about 8½″ long,
   cut crosswise in half
2 tsp. shortening
⅔ C. semi-sweet chocolate chips
Butterscotch-flavored chips, melted

Preheat oven to 350°. In a medium bowl, mix brown sugar, butter, water and vanilla. Stir in flour and salt. Shape dough into twenty 1¼″ balls. Place pretzel rod halves on ungreased cookie sheet. Press dough ball onto cut end of each pretzel rod. Press dough with fork to resemble "bristles" of broom. Bake about 12 minutes or until set, but not brown. Remove from cookie sheet. Cool completely on wire rack for about 30 minutes. Cover cookie sheet with wax paper. Place brooms on wax paper. Heat shortening and chocolate chips over low heat or in microwave, stirring occasionally, until melted and smooth. Spoon melted chocolate over the base of the brooms covering about 1″ of the pretzel handle and the top part of cookie bristles. Drizzle melted butterscotch chips over the chocolate broom base. Let stand until set.

Butterfly Bites

2 stalks celery
12 large twist pretzels
6 T. peanut butter or cream cheese

18 raisins or currants
12 slivered almonds

Wash the celery and cut into thirds. Fill each celery stalk with 1 tablespoon of either peanut butter or cream cheese. For the wings, gently push 2 pretzels into the filling, next to each side and connecting in the middle, running parallel to the length of the celery stick. Arrange the raisins or currants as eyes, nose and mouth. For antennae, push the slivered almonds into filling.

Bumblebee Cookies

½ C. peanut butter
½ C. shortening
⅓ C. brown sugar
⅓ C. honey
1 egg

1¾ C. all-purpose flour
¾ tsp. baking soda
½ tsp. baking powder
96 small pretzel twists
96 small pretzel sticks

In a large bowl, beat peanut butter, shortening, brown sugar, honey and egg with electric mixer on medium speed or mix with a spoon. Stir in flour, baking soda and baking powder. Cover dough with plastic wrap and refrigerate about 2 hours or until firm. Preheat the oven to 350°. Shape dough into 1″ balls (dough will be slightly sticky). For each cookie, place 2 pretzel twists side by side with the bottom touching on ungreased cookie sheet (the bottom is the rounded point, similar to the bottom of a heart shape). Place 1 ball of dough on center; flatten slightly. Break 2 pretzel sticks in half. Gently press 3 pretzel stick halves into dough for stripes on bee. Break fourth pretzel piece in half. Poke pieces into 1 end of dough for antennae. Repeat with remaining dough and pretzels. Bake 11 to 13 minutes or until light golden brown. Remove from cookie sheet to wire rack; cool completely.

Birdhouse Cupcakes

12 paper baking cups
½ C. butter or margarine, softened
¾ C. sugar
1 tsp. ground cinnamon
½ tsp. baking soda
½ tsp. ground nutmeg
½ tsp. vanilla
¼ tsp. salt
2 eggs
1 C. mashed overripe bananas
   (about 3 medium)

1-8 oz. can crushed pineapple in
   juice, well drained
1⅓ C. all-purpose flour
6 T. butter or margarine, softened
1-8 oz. pkg. cream cheese, softened
3½ C. powdered sugar
Green, blue, pink and yellow
   paste (gel) food color
12 thin pretzel sticks
12 semi-sweet chocolate mini Kisses
Tiny flower candies

(continued on next page)

Preheat the oven to 375°. Line 12 muffin cups with baking cups. In a large bowl, heat butter, sugar, cinnamon, baking soda, nutmeg, vanilla and salt with mixer on high speed for 1 minute or until well blended. Add eggs; beat for 2 minutes or until fluffy. Reduce speed to low; beat in bananas and pineapple (batter will look curdled), then add flour just until blended. Spoon into lined muffin cups (they'll be full). Bake 18 to 22 minutes until a toothpick inserted in centers comes out clean. Cool in pan on a wire rack for 5 minutes, then remove cupcakes from pan to rack to cool completely. To make frosting, beat butter, cream cheese and powdered sugar in a large bowl with mixer on low speed until blended. Increase speed to high; beat for 2 minutes or until smooth and fluffy. Tint ¼ cup frosting green and spoon into a plastic bag; set aside. Divide remaining frosting among 3 cups and tint blue, pink and yellow. Cover tightly until ready to use. Peel liners off cupcakes; place on a flat tray. Working with 1 color frosting at a time, drop a heaping teaspoon on 4 cupcakes; spoon remainder into a plastic bag. Snip ⅛″ tip off corner of bag and pipe lines of frosting to simulate thatch for roof. Snip tip off corner of bag with green frosting and pipe grass around base of cupcakes. Insert Kiss (point first) into side of cupcake. Insert pretzel under Kiss; press flowers on grass tops.

Rudolph Cookies

4-1 oz. squares chocolate
  candy coating
96 pretzel sticks

1-16 oz. Nutter Butter cookies
64 blue, green, or brown mini M&M's
32 red mini M&M's

Microwave chocolate candy coating in a small shallow glass dish on high for 3 minutes, stirring once. Insert 2 pretzel sticks in peanut butter filling of each sandwich cookie, forming large antlers. Break remaining pretzel sticks in half and place pretzel halves next to longer pretzel sticks, forming antlers. Dip 1 side of blue, green or brown mini M&M's in melted candy coating and place, coated side down, on cookies for the eyes. Dip 1 side of red mini M&M in candy coating, and place on cookies coated side down, for the nose.

Calico Kitty Cookies

1-18 oz. pkg. refrigerated chocolate
  chip cookie dough
48 pecan halves

72 M&M's
48 thin pretzel sticks, halved

Place cookie dough in freezer for at least 1 hour. Preheat the oven to 350°. Cut cookie dough into 24 slices. Place slices 3″ apart on ungreased cookie sheets. For ears, press 2 pecan halves onto top of each cookie, overlapping edge of cookie. For eyes and nose, press in M&M's. For whiskers, place 2 pretzel halves on each side of nose; press in slightly. Bake 11 to 13 minutes or until golden brown. Cool for 1 minute. Transfer to wire racks to cool completely.

Snowman on a Stick

3 large marshmallows
1 lollipop stick (8˝)
1 peanut butter cup
1 chocolate wafer
Creamy peanut butter

2 pretzel sticks
1 fruit roll up
Decorations, such as miniature
   semi-sweet chocolate chips and
   small candies

Thread marshmallows on lollipop stick to form "snowman." Attach peanut butter cup to chocolate wafer using small amount of peanut butter. Place on top of snowman for "hat." Insert pretzel sticks into middle marshmallow for "arms." Cut fruit roll into desired length for scarf; wrap around snowman. Decorate snowman with chocolate chips and candies as desired.

Index

Dips, Drops & Barks

Sweet Crunchies